Magic Quill, Sacred Sword

Magic Quill, Sacred Sword

Poetic Messages of Divine Spiritual Healing

Janine Palmer (Silver Moon) CHT

– A JP Silver Moon Series –

STONEWALL PRESS
PAVING YOUR WAY TO SUCCESS

Magic Quill, Sacred Sword
Copyright © 2018 by Janine Palmer (Silver Moon) CHT. All rights reserved.

No part of this publication may be reproduced, stored in a retrieval system or transmitted in any way by any means, electronic, mechanical, photocopy, recording or otherwise without the prior permission of the author except as provided by USA copyright law.

The opinions expressed by the author are not necessarily those of Stonewall Press.

Published in the United States of America

ISBN: 978-1-64460-031-3 (*sc*)
      978-1-64460-030-6 (*e*)

Library of Congress Control Number: 2018961680

Published by Stonewall Press
4800 Hampden Lane, Suite 200, Bethesda, MD 20814 USA
1.888.334.0980 | www.stonewallpress.com

Poetry
19.01.04

Other Books by Janine Palmer

MAIN BOOKS

Divine Heretic – Standing Holy
Divine Heretic – In Christ Consciousness
Divine Heretic – Sacred Scribe
Divine Heretic – Mystical Fire
Divine Heretic – Alchemist
Divine Heretic – Hierophant
Divine Heretic – Hidden Keys

GENRE SPECIFIC BOOKS
(Material Pulled from Main Books)

Energy Healing Wisdom
Spiritual Healing Wisdom
Divine Healing Wisdom
Rising Above Dogma
For Romance
Heart Speak
Book of Worthiness
Apocalypse of Worthiness
Scriptures of Worthiness
Shamanic Energy Medicine
Sacred Shamanic Whispers
Fire & Thunder of the Bard

This book is dedicated to my family with deep love and to all the people who inspired me to write and to all poets and writers. The poetry contained herein is an acknowledgement to the healing powers of writing. Writing about the importance of processing and releasing emotions becomes artistic expression. Energy needs to flow. These tales are about releasing those blocks. Trust the process of unfolding and spiritual evolvement.

Blessings, love and light.
Janine Palmer (Silver Moon) CHT

Contents

Foreword 11

Sacred Temple 13
Glimpses of Soul 29
Mystical & Sacred 39
Divine Wisdom 49
Energy Healing 59
Fire of Transformation 73
Spiritual Alchemy 81
Worthiness & Wings 99
Blessed Be Our Magic 107
Deeper Truth 117
Mirror, Mirror 129
Battle Scars & Shedding Skins 141
Treasure & Keys 153
Suffering & Shadow 165
Whispers from the Heart 183
Light through the Cracks 193
Spoken from the Soul 203
Beyond Belief 215
Metaphoric Light 225
Perspectives 231

Foreword

THIS LITTLE BOOK REFLECTS GLIMPSES of experience and the wisdom gained from them. It reflects wounds, and the effects of the wounded who wound. It speaks of energy healing and forgiveness. It speaks of spiritual alchemy and the ascension of the spirit and the soul. It speaks of opening the door of the heart to love.

It speaks of battle scars and shedding skins and shells. It speaks of sacred temples and the fire of transformation. It speaks of rising above and moving beyond judgment, the spiraling, higher path to freedom through love and healing and releasing what does not serve. It speaks of the power of forgiveness. It speaks of things mystical and sacred. It speaks of magic.

It speaks of angels and dragons and divine love. It speaks of mirrors, treasures, keys and the mystical. It speaks of shadow and perspectives. It speaks of spirit, heart, soul and light. It speaks of deeper truth beyond belief and hidden keys. It basically shares the depth of love revealed by life experiences.

Sacred Temple

You are your own guide,
who is always guided by
aspects of love.

Sacred Temple

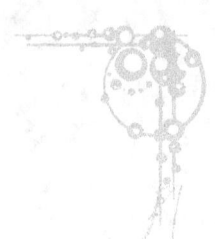

She sat among the mists reflecting on what had been painful and misunderstood. It was time to release it to higher source so she could rise above it and heal, which would help the collective to rise and heal as well.

Sacred Temple

My spark was kindled into a roaring flame of sacred grace.

Sacred Temple

He walked the mysterious hall ways which led to the garden of my heart. He had to clear away a few cobwebs of neglect. He felt something in my soul he recognized. He helped to fill my vessel and nurtured the love that grows there. My heart remembered him and welcomed him home.

Sacred Temple

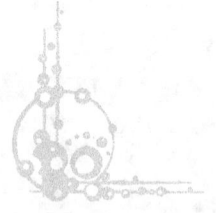

My friend posed the question, 'What is Love?'

My limited answer is: 'Love is the highest pure essence we were created from that is always part of us, which is beautiful and compassionate beyond description when we feel it, know it, and share through grace.

It is what allows us to give even when it seems we have nothing to give. We are never without it, even if sometimes we don't recognize or remember it. It's a gift. It's our gift.

It's our strength. Sometimes love is what saves us from everything else, which is illusion. The absence of it might be what we call evil, which is ignorance. To be ignorant of love is to suffer.

Love is far stronger than fear but we must reconnect with it. Love without expectations. Love which creates. Love which heals. Love can heal us and we can heal by sharing love with others.

This is the important role animals play in our lives by how healing they can be for us and what they can teach us about unconditional love.'

My friend said love is about the Mystery, reverence and awe, which we often lose by trying to label things and place them in a box of (limited) understanding.

(Thank you Marilyn for posing this excellent question)

Sacred Temple

Scars tell important
stories about events
which transform us.

Sacred Temple

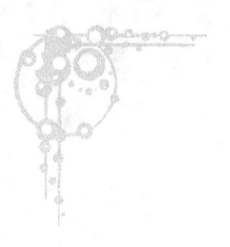
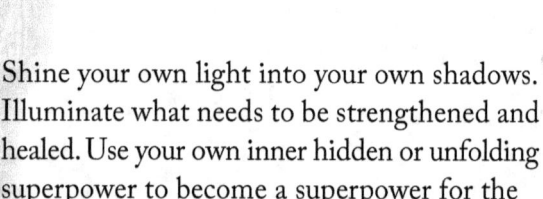

Shine your own light into your own shadows. Illuminate what needs to be strengthened and healed. Use your own inner hidden or unfolding superpower to become a superpower for the greater good of the collective world.

Fill yourself with so much love that the negativity of anyone else cannot penetrate your sacred, radiant armor of light and if it did it would instantly be transmuted into love, the love which resides in you.

Sacred Temple

It might be time to remember, recall or recognize the love in you that is you. Tools to assist you with this might be calmness, detachment, forgiveness, calling in angels, prayer, meditation, spending time in nature, reflection, letting go of expectations, jealousy, resentment, wrath, anger, blame, sadness, guilt, shame and grief, and filling yourself up with love and let it shine like the sun.

Sacred Temple

Broken heartedness does not or should not define us. We shouldn't identify with it so much that we become that thing or that idea of something, which is limited and limiting. It might be part of an experience from which we were meant to learn. It might be an idea of what we thought something was or was supposed to be. It might be attached to expectations about something and it is said having expectations is like making an agreement for someone without their permission.

When we are in relationship with someone, they are having a different experience than we are. They have their own fears, old wounds, ghosts, walls, etc., which direct them or hold them back. To try to have the kind of relationship you think you want with someone who doesn't feel the same might be empty, lacking, lonely, frustrating or torturous. It might be reflecting to us the need for detachment and the opportunity to learn it. Attachment causes suffering. We even have attachment to ideas about things.

This world is about change and growth and about creation and destruction. Our hearts need to be healed and they need to be loved… by ourselves. If we go around continually thinking and saying we have a broken heart then that is what we create and our heart probably doesn't like it. Yes, it might feel broken, we've all experienced something like that. It's how we move past it that is the test. Sometimes it's the thoughts about it that are broken, not the heart.

Maybe it would be better not to give so much power away from our sacred heart space by feeling or thinking that we cannot function or recover. Thought forms like these, which feed programs, not only keep people stuck, they can eventually create illness or dis – ease. Change your thoughts, change your life. What would happen if we stopped identifying with the negative? The organs in our body would certainly be happier and healthier.

We have many energy centers in the body. Energy must flow. We create blocks in these energy centers when we continue to focus on or lament about things being other than we had hoped. Negative thoughts about things create energetic entities which stick to our energy field and they need to be fed by the thoughts we continually think. Sometimes illness presents as a result of what we carry and have not released.

We should not carry or bury, sadness, guilt, shame, blame, grief, guilt, anger, resentment anger or unforgiveness. They can rule or destroy if we allow them to. These 'unfortunate' events in our lives are tests which are inviting us to learn how to take our power back. We can change our relationship to anything, even our thoughts or perspectives about things, so we are not prisoners or slaves to things.

We can visualize pulling the energy of something out of ourselves, thanking it for what we learned, and then imagine getting rid of it however we choose. Release what doesn't serve you and send yourself love and healing. So many of us have an inner child which is in need of acknowledgment, healing and a massive amount of love that only we can give it.

It's not up to anyone else to make us happy, that is an inside job. No one else can make us unhappy unless we allow them to. We have the choice of whether to stand in our power or give it away. A lot of the time we don't realize we are giving our power away and we don't know exactly which parts of us require healing. This is why mediation is so helpful for healing on so many levels, emotional, mental, spiritual and physical.

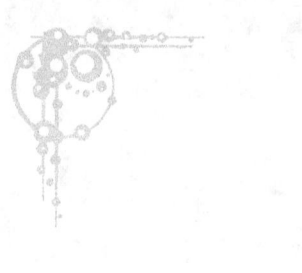
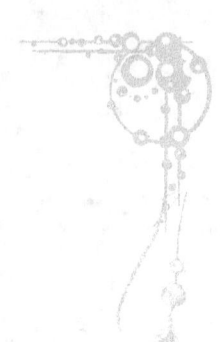

Every day is an opportunity for you to create what you want rather than staying in a stagnant energy which feels like hell. Ask higher source to help you to heal in whatever way it's needed. Love yourself first.

Sacred Temple

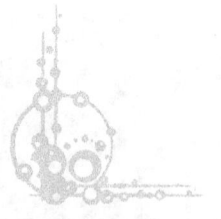

Glimpses of Soul

There were aspects of the queen unknown or unremembered. They were compassionate aspects known to many at the time of her reign, but forgotten in history except for what had been written in diaries and journals by those who were touched by her kindness.

Glimpses of Soul

No matter how intuitive we are, or what we think we know about anyone, there are aspects and agreements about people that we simply do not know. Things which might not be revealed to us which are extremely relevant. We do not know what trauma(s) a being has experienced, in this life or before. We do not know what they brought in with them which needs to be healed, which still tests them.

We might have agreed to be guides, reminders, teachers, family, friends or tests. But judgment and unkindness never serve anyone here, unless it's by learning from the pain caused by it, not to do it to others. Sometimes directness or honesty is misinterpreted as unkindness by those with unhealed wounds or expectations. What we focus our thoughts on, we create and draw into our experiences, even and especially fears. Facing fear and moving beyond it is very powerful.

We do not and cannot know everything about anyone on this plane. We all stumble in our efforts to remember our magnificence and worthiness, as we move beyond ignorance and illusion. Look at your hands. Do they help people up or do they push them down? Do they need to be washed? Do they need love? Do they give love? What we give comes back to us. If we judge others we keep ourselves trapped in our own unhealed wounds. Love yourself first.

Glimpses of Soul

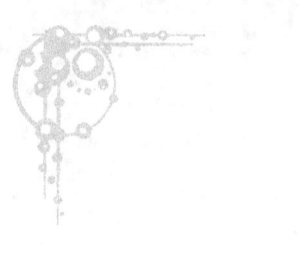

He didn't take from me anything I wasn't willing to give. I gave him my love willingly. It couldn't be any other way, because my soul recognized him and welcomed him home.

Glimpses of Soul

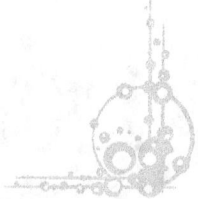

It got to the point that I was so drained, that I was too tired to fight. There was no more energy he could take. It assisted me in disconnecting from what absolutely did not serve me or my calling. My efforts at refining the power of detachment moved up a notch to the level of Master.

Glimpses of Soul

I stayed with him even though I experienced emotional and mental neglect or abuse, which he probably was not fully aware he inflicted or which he would never want to admit. I stayed when I felt empty, alone, misunderstood, judged and shut out. Even when I left for periods of time, I came back. There are things we do or don't do which even our conscious minds don't understand.

The heart and the soul guide us. Tests strengthen and prepare us. I knew he was hurt and doing his best, even if he was stuck in patterns, habits, non-communication and not facing things. I couldn't fix him and he couldn't fix me. We must look after ourselves, and then things will come into alignment. No expectations. No attachment. No resentment. No blame. Love of self. Healing self. A good place to start.

Glimpses of Soul

We want people to sing to our soul,
to bring us back home...but everyone
is wounded.

Glimpses of Soul

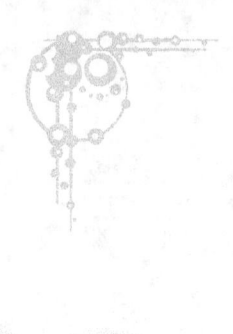

She wondered how much of a person's inability to communicate came from their brokenness, and what did it need to take for a person to endeavor to fix it?

Glimpses of Soul

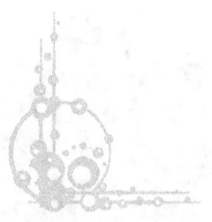
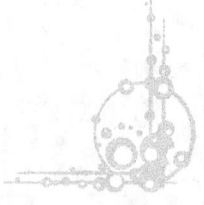

Mystical & Sacred

She sat before a shattered mirror
with two white ravens. The ravens
came to tell her the mirror was
shattered because she didn't need
it anymore. She had healed all it had
reflected back to her. It was time to
clear the cobwebs.

Mystical & Sacred

Under the hood of her elegant cloak,
Was a priestess here in disguise,
Hidden from view from the many,
From the realm where whispers fly.

Whispers of wisdom remembered,
Cutting away ignorance's threads,
Balance through completeness and worthiness,
As recognition drives out false dread.

The flower that he handed her,
Represented the fragrance of love's ancient story,
And the kiss she placed upon his cheek,
Created unseen sparks from sacred glory.

Mystical & Sacred

The beat of the drum took her to other worlds where deep healing took place with the help of many beloved guides.

Mystical & Sacred

His laugh warmed my heart with the welcome feeling of home.

Mystical & Sacred

My adopted son in Africa asked a question when we were discussing God, 'Who is God? How do you know who is God?'

I answered, I think God is something we can't understand with our human conscious mind. I feel we are of God. We are all sparks of God or we have the sparks of God in us but some of us don't recognize it yet. Some of haven't discovered it yet. Some of us haven't awakened to it yet.

Some religions program us to feel unworthy because people worship a god that is not complete, a god that requires things from humanity to sustain itself. Some people do not even realize what they worship, so they become stuck. God is in the messages. Prophets and books point to God, which is within everyone.

There are messages from or about God in books which come through prophets, but there are parts that are tweaked, misinterpreted, mistranslated, perverted and otherwise misunderstood. Just observe the state of the world. Observation is key.

How powerful we are when we can observe without reacting, without becoming slaves to things, people, Ideologies, religions, politics, books, fears or misperceptions.

There are things of this world which are simply tools which might be used in different ways by the person holding the tool. If it works for one person's ultimate purpose or goal, who is to say whether how that person uses a tool is right or wrong? It's all about perception and misperception.

We all learn from things which are labeled right or wrong or good or bad. Perhaps the key is not to get stuck on one chapter or page of the book and not to worship the prophet because in doing so, we might not truly see, hear, feel, remember, or know God.

God is the helping hand that gives food or water to a starving or thirsty animal or person. A kind word, a hug, a listening ear. Functioning in the absence of judgment, jealousy or anger. That is God working through people. It's the kindness. It's the love and compassion humanity expresses, that is God. It's the kindness. It's love.

Mystical & Sacred

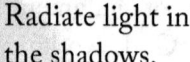

Radiate light in
the shadows.

Mystical & Sacred

Divine Wisdom

If you have a question,
ask. Don't assume,

Divine Wisdom

Compassion, while mysteriously powerful and transformative, can get one harmed or killed, because the light functions in dignity, integrity and grace. Darkness has no rules which govern it except ignorance and wanting power to fill its incompleteness, which has spawned jealousy, anger, wrath and other similar energies or behaviors connected lower vibrational tools of suffering.

Misperceptions are a huge culprit in this, when people view things through the lens of their woundedness and then endeavor to judge and attack due to vindictiveness, fear and limited, inaccurate or incomplete information. Ego and pride often direct this. When these lower aspects are no longer in charge one can begin to take their power back and create something of a higher, healthier vibration.

Darkness, through ignorance and incompleteness, which either cannot see the light or sees it and wants to destroy it in its jealousy, destroys everything in its path and eventually will include itself. Darkness will create its own demise. When people are caught up in the grip or snare of these energies, creating more and more harm and destruction, the only way to escape it or over power it, is to forgive it and rise above it. Send love.

Divine Wisdom

All darkness sees is itself. It is blinded by its own ignorance and incompleteness or by its jealousy and wrath. Not knowing how to complete itself, it sets out on a path of destruction through fear and control. It will ultimately destroy itself.

Keep shining your divine light to illuminate the darkness as you begin to remember your completeness, which has been hidden from you. To disengage from the effects of darkness and ignorance you must step out of the box and question all beliefs. You must break out of the cocoon of illusion to discover your hidden wings.

The darkness hides much, but it cannot hide your light from you forever. Your divinity will reveal itself to you and compassion is a master key.

Divine Wisdom

Things are only as
complicated as we
make them.

Divine Wisdom

What is the energy of God? What is the unfolding understanding of God, which isn't only Him, or Her? There often comes a time to stop worshiping 'books' which only point toward God. God isn't only in a book. God (Love) is in everything and everyone. Or maybe that depends on what god people worship, if they really even know.

Does their god require them to take sides or to feel unworthy? Maybe it's time to upgrade perceptions and perspectives. It might be extremely helpful to stop worshiping books and prophets because we don't and can't know God truly only through them. People are the Word. We are the pages of the Book.

This is why teachers come into our lives because they will teach us things every day, if we are open enough to learn. I learn from you, maybe you learn from me. But we must blast out of the programs in our minds that we run which also run us. The greatest lesson might be to learn to love yourself again which always includes forgiveness. Through that reinstatement of truth, we (re)discover God within.

Divine Wisdom

We are always learning and we
are always meant to be learning.
If we are not always learning, then
we might stay stuck in stagnation
and that's not what we're meant to do.

As we continue to learn, our
perspectives continue to change.
If we stay stuck in perceptions we
think we must defend, it might be
coming from our pain body, ego,
fear or programming.

Divine Wisdom

Energy Healing

When a person can take responsibility for what they create(d), they can then change what they create(d) which they don't like or which doesn't serve them.

Energy Healing

Elevation

Ego's attachment to the trauma,
Not letting go of the cords to pain,
Keeps many stuck under a dark cloud,
Drenched in recurring thoughts like rain.

If only they were thoughts which cleanse us,
If only they shut old programs down,
If only they incinerated the cords and shackles,
Which make us dance like puppet clowns.

Rise above the trauma now,
For the experience of a different view,
For the experience of transformation,
Which is wanting to come through.

Ego's attachment to the trauma,
Is something to be released like a balloon to the wind,
It's something to be overcome through opening,
As we unfold to begin again.

Energy Healing

Sometimes how people view things is perceived through or perverted by unhealed pain. Sometimes people attack or lash out at others when in reality in some way, they might be attacking what they have not healed or released in themselves. Things appear as and are created by false perspectives. False thoughts, perspectives and beliefs are often connected to unhealed wounds and the wounded inner child, which might create a warped reality.

Fear attracts fear, love attracts love. Love is your experience of God. Move into love. God experiences itself through mankind. What are you creating for God to experience? Masters choose only love for it is the strongest power there is and it is above all else.

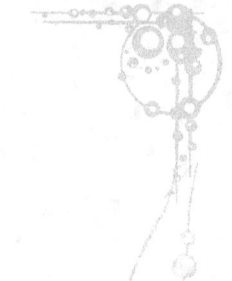

Life is a process of choices by which we allow ourselves to be pulled down, due to perceptions, or to stay stuck, due to perceptions, or rise above and beyond perceptions when we no longer allow them to rule us. To get there we must strengthen weakness and heal wounds, and we do it through love and forgiveness. Forgiveness of the illusion.

Energy Healing

People carry energy, even in the form of thoughts, which need to be processed and released, that they often don't even realize are there.

Happiness is a choice, however, a person might carry energy which causes them to feel unhappy, typically related to thoughts about things which are loops which feed or run programs.

They are not aware of what it is our how to heal it or release it. We learn from everything and everyone. We create by thought and choice.

Energy Healing

Everyone is intuitive to different degrees, depending on if or how they recognize it. How they use it is what matters. It is a gift. Some use it for good purpose, others do not. Some offer messages, guidance and wisdom for healing and forward movement. Some, who read or sense, energy, use wounds or fears against people, which only reflect the wounds or fears of the one who is misusing their 'gifts'.

Everything is for our learning. We learn from all of it. Perhaps we draw experiences in to test ourselves. If there is an unresolved issue somewhere in our energy field, situations will continue to present until we strengthen weakness, heal wounds and rise above.

There is much that is known and unknown, seen and unseen. We are all in the process of spiritual evolvement and we must do inner work in order to ascend. Learn from people, but don't hold their shadow aspects against them or it might keep you stuck. Don't hold your shadow aspects against yourself either, even though there are those who would attempt to use them against you. It's all a test for us to learn through experience.

It okay to step away from people and away from their patterns and habits which attempt to draw you into lower energies. It's okay to distance yourselves from those who disrespect you and treat you unkindly, even if it's only due to perspectives or misperspectives.

If it feels wrong or bad or doesn't flow with grace, move on, walk away, rise above and send love. You honor yourself when you do not allow others to dishonor you, but you don't need to hold it against them as that is a trap. Move on in peace.

Clear your space. Don't let anyone to remain in your energetic space if they can't do so in honor and grace. People often go into old patterns and habits of their unhealed wounds often from their wounded inner child. It's up to them to determine how and when to address that and heal it. It's not okay for them to work out their issues on you.

If a person causes you to feel upset or attacked, then it's for your own well-being to disengage. Sometimes feeling triggered or upset might actually be reflecting your own unhealed wounded and issues. Sometimes people feel offended due to ego. Part of the test is discovering what is making you 'feel' or react a certain way. Where do the roots to it go? Where do they come from? But if you can definitely tell that what is transpiring has nothing to do with you and you just don't want it in your space, cut cords, clear yourself of the toxic energy and give yourself permission to move on. You're not being unkind. It is self-care.

Energy Healing

The labels we throw at someone who hurt us might be relevant terminology which describes their behaviors, which usually stem from unhealed or unresolved wounds or issues, theirs or ours.

We might come to the awareness of this through the heinous ways we were treated and how it wounded us terribly. So is it possible then, that through our wounds, and not knowing how to release and heal them, that we also become that?

Do we become the things we label and attack because that is what attacked us and knocked us into another, lower dimension? We might become that from wounds, known or unknown, just as the person who wounded us became that from wounds. Wounded people wound people.

If you don't heal, you suffer. If you don't heal, you take it with you until you learn from it, but you might hurt others along the way. We can have awareness of something and discuss is for learning and healing and release…but is it laced with bitterness? Do we hear or see or feel the bitterness that glares through from our tone, what we say or don't say, what we write, what we judge, what we attack?

Bitterness is related to attachment to something, to judging it, to resentment, to unreleased anger, to pain. Those emotional and mental energies should not be left to fester within or they can eventually cause physical dis-ease.

Can we learn from the experience and let the rest go? Are we defined by any negative experience? Maybe we are, until we rise about it, and that is the test. Is something painful we experienced, now our identity? Maybe, until we take our power back from it.

Anytime we cease to relate to any wounded, lower vibrational, tainted, twisted, warped thing, we can begin to find the truth of ourselves again, not just who we think they turned us into. It's always choice. Thoughts must be changed to create a new and better and healthier reality. Old, negative thought forms feed old, negative programs that you run or they run you.

When you discuss it or write about it, can you also show and share something positive you learned from it? Things unhealed and unresolved can be healed and resolved in silence and mediation and forgiveness. There are so many ways you can step out onto the path of your own healing and empowerment. Are you ready to take your power back from anyone or anything? You can be free whenever you choose to be.

Energy Healing

Fire of Transformation

He wasn't happy but he wasn't prepared to do anything to change it. The bottle ruled him. The wounds ruled him. Fear ruled.

It's all choice. If you don't like something, make a different choice. You're the creator of your own reality.

It's amazing what happens when you nurture love with love rather than closing off due to fear, slow cooking in the juices of unhealed wounds.

What power has love?

Fire of Transformation

Illuminate your own mystery.

Fire of Transformation

Many candles will light your
path and your light will light
many candles.

Fire of Transformation

To surrender is to release the illusion of control whereby you come into your own power.

Fire of Transformation

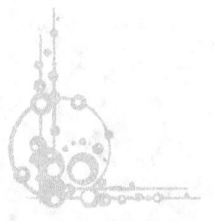

I learned from an amazing
spiritual teacher that the
behavior of others, what
other people do or say, is
not a reflection of you, it's
a direct reflection of them.
Your response to what others
do is a reflection of you.

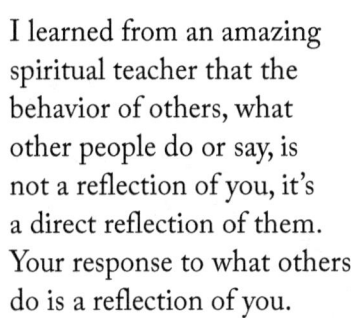

Fire of Transformation

Spiritual Alchemy

Burn the 'Cards'…

We have all been persecuted on some level or to some degree in this life or another. We have all been slaves, slaves to something or someone, in this life or another, probably due to amnesia and forgetting our worthiness. We have all suffered in similar and different ways, understood or misunderstood, known or unknown, seen or unseen, felt or not felt.

No one holds that exclusive 'card', to be waved around to make one feel more wounded or more important than anyone else. Depending on what you know, believe or remember, that person you are attacking for something that happened to your ancestors might very well be the spirit of one of those ancestors.

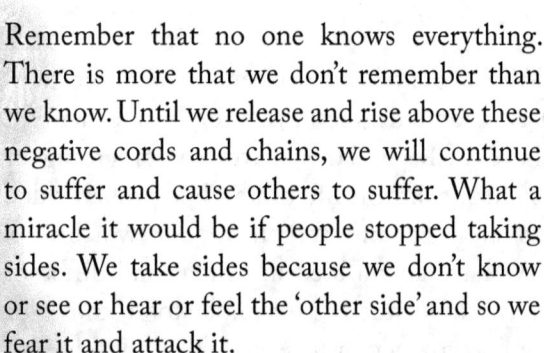

Remember that no one knows everything. There is more that we don't remember than we know. Until we release and rise above these negative cords and chains, we will continue to suffer and cause others to suffer. What a miracle it would be if people stopped taking sides. We take sides because we don't know or see or hear or feel the 'other side' and so we fear it and attack it.

Maybe it's time to throw the 'cards' into the fire, along with the labels and false sense of superiority. Maybe it's time for baptism by fire, transformation by fire, or purification by fire—the fires we were forged in but have forgotten in a lower vibrational, often hellish, abusive, wounded plane.

You are love. It's where you came from and it is in you. If you share it with yourself and others, along with the super power of forgiveness, you would see a world changing for the positive. What is your gift of love and how do you or can you or will you share it?

Spiritual Alchemy

So often we sacrifice ourselves to save others. When we become weaker, they become stronger.

When you let go of saving others and face your anger toward them, you might realize you're angry with yourself for letting the ego think it would be a hero.

We need to be our own hero in our own lives to become independent and strong in ourselves.

Spiritual Alchemy

One day she decided she had learned enough from the experiences of persecution, so she wrote them out of her story and wrote in more abundance of love.

Spiritual Alchemy

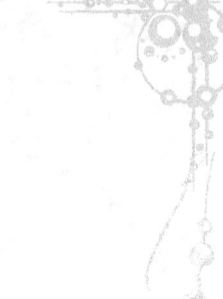

Sometimes in order to heal or move forward you need to change your thoughts about things, because many of our thoughts aren't even true, but they feed the programs we run, or the programs which run and control us. Change your thoughts, change your life, stop the unnecessary suffering.

Spiritual Alchemy

Many speak about what the cross means, or has meant through the millennia, even before it came to be used as certain symbols today or over the past two thousand years. A friend shared a deep and profound analogy with me which I had also come across previously when studying Biblical scholars. However metaphoric, it will have different meaning to different people, depending on their current level of awakening and awareness or programming and conditioning. It will depend on how open or closed they currently are.

I say currently because perspectives and perceptions are always changing, or should be, as knowledge comes into our field of awareness and as we begin to awaken to or remember deeper, forgotten truths. It will have much more meaning to the true seeker and probably not as much to those comfortably existing behind the walls of their particular boxes. Walls, however flimsy or strong, are designed to keep things in or out, which might obstruct the flow of knowledge, learning, growing, healing, awakening and ascending.

Here is basically what my friend shared: The metaphoric meaning of the cross or crucifix is sometimes understood as a symbol of the final crossing out of any sense of separation on a soul level (the death and dying to the ego self), in total surrender of resurrection and ascension into a new level of consciousness. So many seem to be programmed to think or 'believe' they are separate from God and somehow unworthy. That comes from ignorance. That is darkness, or ignorance, working through religions. When you begin to realize that God is in you and in everyone and everything around you, you begin to rise.

Scriptural stories and teachings are metaphoric. We are meant to read between the lines, to discover the deeper spiritual meaning they contain. They are not meant to bolster, feed or encourage egoic bickering and soldering for positions considered 'right'. That is something different for each person depending, as stated above, on their particular level of awakening and awareness and on how open or closed they are due to their experiences, wounds, levels of healing, levels of understanding, programming, conditioning, thought forms etc.

When we disengage from controlling entities which direct and control through fear then we can begin to come into contact with more truthful aspects of who we really are. When we realize how falsehoods have been used to shackle us, and endeavor to walk out of our self-made cells, we shall rejoice through the grace which is always part of us.

We exist here in a free will zone. We create our reality by choice, however, outside sources might have influenced us or what we might have adopted as truth. Truth is always within. We can change our lives by changing our thoughts and our choices. To become empty might create space for light to re-enter and to emerge. Peace.

Spiritual Alchemy

It was after a series of unfortunate events I didn't 'understand', that I learned something extremely valuable from a spiritual teacher. I learned that when people are unkind or unfair to me, if I remain in a place of not 'understanding' it and feeling hurt by it, I'm judging it. I had no idea that was the case. I can be aware that something is 'wrong', or incompatible for my energy, but I don't need to stay around and try to correct by pointing it out and arguing. I just need to recognize it, bless it, let it go and move away from it.

I didn't realize that by talking about or thinking about how jacked up it was, I was judging it. When we judge we are withholding love from ourselves. I noticed when others judged people in ways that were unnecessary or unfair and I would often write or teach as a reminder not to judge. When you think, assume or say that someone is wrong when you haven't had their experience, or you don't have all the information, it can create problems. But there is another kind of judgment.

When someone tells someone else that you did something which you absolutely did not do, and you hear about it and it hurts or offends, if you can't find a way to rise above it, and continue to feel hurt by it, you're judging it and by doing that you're withholding love from yourself. Or, when someone targets you and projects on you and attacks you and you don't 'understand' why.

It's a challenge and a choice to just remove yourself from it. Bless them and send yourself love. Stay away from friends with energy that doesn't serve you which you cannot 'fix'. You must move away from it for your own well-being. To feel hurt by what you do not or cannot understand, it a type of judgment. It's all a test. Relationships are tests.

Spiritual Alchemy

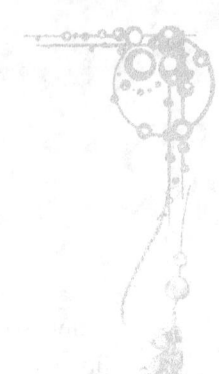

I finally discovered I needed to say to myself, 'I'm sorry I didn't love you correctly and directly. I'm sorry I didn't know how. I'm sorry I thought I needed someone else to do that. I'm sorry for when I gave too much to others and not enough to you.'

Spiritual Alchemy

It took me a long time to shift certain things to make a needed difference in my life. Glimpses of light came from others who were able to deliver messages in a way that I would receive it. After suffering and struggle from misperception, I needed a change in perspective. I had to learn to view things differently in order to have a different experience.

Spiritual Alchemy

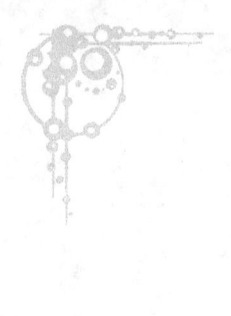

It was amazing to get to a place where I didn't care. Not through any type of depression, but through power.

The power of calmness and detachment. The power of knowing, remembering, loving and honoring myself and raising my vibration.

Spiritual Alchemy

We learn from the struggles or through them. The struggles cease when we learn what we are meant to learn. Something in us shifts when we have a certain breakthrough of deeper understanding or realization through a different perspective and through honest reflection.

Sometimes something we hear or read or experience just clicks. The penny drops and something shifts. Something makes sense to such a different degree that we can now move away from what was holding us back. Then we can shed the cloak we carried which was worn and useless.

Spiritual Alchemy

Worthiness & Wings

He didn't seem to fathom how she had rearranged her life to be part of his. He let her in and loved her quietly, so quietly she almost didn't feel it. The quietness of non-communication and non-interaction.

Perhaps after being in a cocoon of disconnect and loneliness for so long, it was time to unfold her wings and fly, to experience the love all around her.

Worthiness & Wings

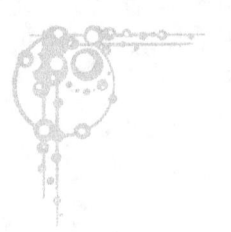
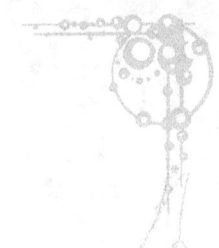

It was almost like she didn't know herself anymore, reflected by the way he almost held her back due to his own unhealed pain and his inability to demonstrate and share love due to fear and protection.

When she disengaged from him, she began to reconnect to parts of herself. Detachment can be a powerful key. Expectation can be a trap.

She began to carve her own path. Her love and compassion was meant to be shared, not stifled or ignored. To break out the shell is birth or rebirth.

Worthiness & Wings

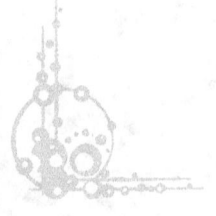

It seemed he would rather find ways to put her down about than embrace her and make her feel loved. Fear is a greedy bastard.

Worthiness & Wings

I came to love and accept myself beyond all outward judgement.

Worthiness & Wings

Gifts are what we make from
what we have, how we honor
them and how we care for them.
Our actions and perspectives
create the gifts.

Worthiness & Wings

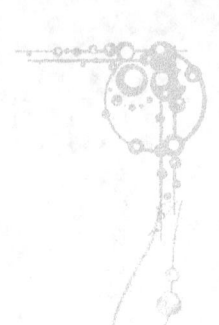

Certain perspectives, when we are ready to be open to them, are like golden keys of light to crack us open to move out of stuckness. Rebirthing new aspects from old shells or cocoons.

Worthiness & Wings

Blessed Be Our Magic

She said, "I think I'll go back to being a Druid next time."

He said, "You never stopped being one," and smiled.

Blessed Be Our Magic

The fingerprints you left
upon my heart were etched
in sacred flame.

Blessed Be Our Magic

Let the misperceptions flow like tears,
through the mists of illusion, creating
a trail back to whence you came, back
to grace and love, through grace and love.

Blessed Be Our Magic

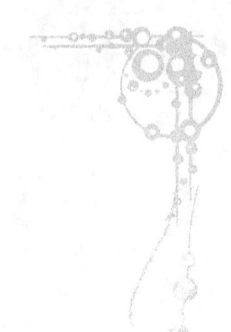

When his wounded child could no longer draw her in to get attention, he had to learn to find a way to heal it if he wanted to stop destroying his relationships.

Blessed Be Our Magic

When she stopped allowing him to manipulate her and left him to his own devices, he began to see the old unshed skin of something unpleasant he hadn't wanted to deal with before. The time to deal with it and fix it had come.

Blessed Be Our Magic

Our choices direct our path. We are drawn or directed to what we are meant to experience or accomplish, often in ways others don't quite understand. Most people don't consciously choose suffering. Sometimes it's simply a change in perspective which stops suffering.

So often we react to thoughts about things, things we didn't understand from a limited perspective. Sometimes we think we suffer(ed) due to someone else, due to misunderstandings, old wounds being triggered, etc.

Sometimes we feel lack in our lives simply because we are not giving ourselves enough love. We give so much to others, but we forget about ourselves. Love is magic. Love is in us and all around us. Remember to love your inner child.

Blessed Be Our Magic

If we strengthen our weaknesses and heal our own wounds, the narcissist can't hurt us. I've learned to not react to it anymore. I've learned not get drawn in. I've learned not to carry or hold onto resentment. I have awareness of it. I recognize it.

I no longer need to judge it. To judge it is to continue to feel hurt by it. That is my power. It took me many years and many difficult lessons to learn to stand in my power. It is an ongoing process of healing and release and it cannot be done without great love.

Blessed Be Our Magic

Deeper Truth

Don't forget that patterns, yours or theirs, create your or their reality. You or they can't always blame everyone else for things.

Deeper Truth

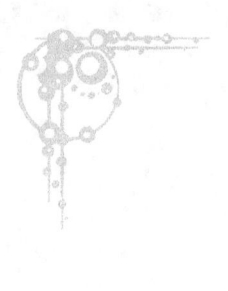

Sometimes, just by trying to be loving and attentive, certain parental figures create little emperors who seem to think it's a women's job to coddle and serve them, and that somehow they don't have to give the same consideration back to the woman. They just drain the vessel without refilling it and wonder why it's empty.

Deeper Truth

Maybe it was just that he didn't know how to approach her or didn't feel comfortable communicating with her because their energies or vibrations were so different. To open is often to rise.

Deeper Truth

They both loved her in different ways,
but never could either own her. How can
anyone own what belongs to the collective?

And only through suffering is it shown.
When something comes to you freely,
it is a gift. When it is forced through false
power or resistance, it will break away.

Deeper Truth

Sometimes the labels we throw around are a description of behaviors we recognize which have harmed us.

Sometimes the labels we throw around are our own behaviors we don't recognize in ourselves.

Only openness and honesty with ourselves will reveal how it applies.

Deeper Truth

He said, "I wish you were
still the woman I married."

Her unspoken response,
'Oh, the one who was asleep
and controllable?'

Parts of us will always be present,
but we didn't come here to stay
the same. We came here to learn
through experience for our souls
to evolve. Everything in this realm
changes. Flow or be dragged.

(Thank you Dorian for your
contribution to this)

Deeper Truth

No onlooker, no matter how intuitive, knows what has challenged anyone in this life, therefore they cannot judge. They may try but would be incorrect in their judgment, lacking valuable, relevant information.

People might be able to see how someone is stuck in ways that other person is not aware of. We might see 'bad' habits other people engage in and want to step in and try to correct them, but they don't need to be put down just because they haven't figured out how rise above the pitfalls of their losses and wounds. Not everybody is fully aware that much or most of what we react to is illusion or misperception.

We probably don't know why people do or don't do things. When we think someone is being unkind or bashing someone else, we probably don't know of the pain or abuse they endured which created what we see or think we see. Just because someone hasn't healed from abuse, it doesn't give them the right to abuse anyone else.

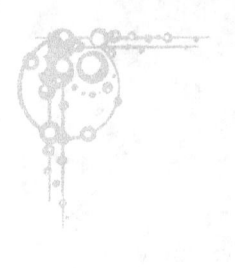

Of course we should step up for what we think is right, even without all the pertinent information. We should always act with integrity and compassion, but not everyone identifies with that, especially if they are suffering. There is always a reason behind a behavior, which we usually don't know. Be kind.

Deeper Truth

Maybe his lack of communication, which seemed like such a stumbling block, was a gift because it caused me to learn more about myself when he wouldn't allow me interact and learn directly through him by what was accepted or not accepted, through feedback and reflection.

My attempts at communication, were mostly just not accepted, so I had to discover myself through myself and not through another. Although, others have helped greatly along the way to help me to know myself better. We are on a journey of remembering... our worthiness.

Deeper Truth

The truth isn't always
what it appears to be.

Deeper Truth

Mirror, Mirror

Oh, you were abused in some way? Some people say, 'Just get over it'. = Disrespect. People are not their stories. The effects of experiences must be processed and released. People should not make their story or their wounds part of their identity, even though it has shaped who they are. Wisdom is meant to be shared.

Sharing the wisdom gained is part of the healing process and it is often helpful to others. It's called transmutation, alchemy and creating something good from something bad, in this illusionary realm of duality. It is part of spiritual unfoldment and there always seems to be someone who wants to attack it.

Mirror, Mirror

What made you do what
you did to someone you
supposedly cared about?
And now it's my task to
Transmute that spiritual
lead into gold.

Mirror, Mirror

Aspects of wisdom woven
and shared, glimpsed or not,
depending on how wide the
door to the heart is open.

Mirror, Mirror

He didn't express love openly to her because he'd been hurt before. She came to help him heal, but he couldn't seem to give back and refill the vessel. He hid for protection. Perhaps he thought if it didn't work out he'd save face because he didn't put himself out there to fail or lose.

But what he failed to realize is that he lost every year the connection crumbled and died in starvation into a shell that was cracking into dust, emptiness and loneliness because he refused to feed it show the love he had received and accepted from her. The love he quietly buried.

Or maybe he just never learned how to treat a woman and she loved him enough to put up without those little things which lift the heart and soul.

Nurture and water what you want to survive and grow.

Mirror, Mirror

It's difficult to tell if his kindness is genuine or contrived for ulterior motives and purposes.

Then there's that moment when you see through the mask and become a distant observer.

We are drawn to what nurtures us or what we're going to learn from.

Mirror, Mirror

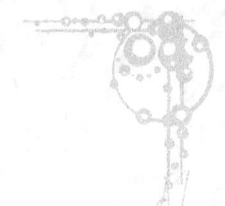

How does taking sides help global peace? How does slamming anyone for their ignorance or limited information, from your ignorance or limited information, help global peace and healing?

We have sides due to our perspectives and beliefs to date, which differ from others. But to lash out and attack from lower energies is like being in a jail cell where people love to fling poo.

Mirror, Mirror

It's difficult to trust when we've been hurt, when wounded people manipulate, expect, attack and twist things around and try to use what matters to us, against us. If we didn't also have wounds it wouldn't hurt as much. What is it trying to show us on a deeper level? It's all a test, but it's never easy.

We must pay very close attention to behaviors as mirrors, to discover whether someone is showing us something in ourselves which needs healing or if they are projecting their issues at us, which still might trigger our own unresolved issues.

When we strengthen weaknesses and heal wounds, other people's obnoxious behaviors won't hurt or affect us so negatively. It they are disrespectful, we don't allow have them in our space. Lessons, for both.

Mirror, Mirror

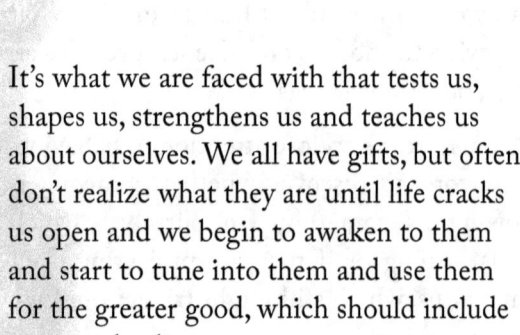

It's what we are faced with that tests us, shapes us, strengthens us and teaches us about ourselves. We all have gifts, but often don't realize what they are until life cracks us open and we begin to awaken to them and start to tune into them and use them for the greater good, which should include our own healing.

Mirror, Mirror

We learn so much through mirroring, when we realize and understand what it is, and not only by reflection, but by projection and to be able to recognize the difference.

It's important to learn from triggers and reactions, our own and others. To release and walk away from what doesn't serve us. To honor ourselves and others through healthy boundaries.

It doesn't serve us or another person to allow them to treat us poorly. It's a test to love ourselves more and to stand in our power, and of course the manipulators aren't going to like it, but that's just too damn bad.

Mirror, Mirror

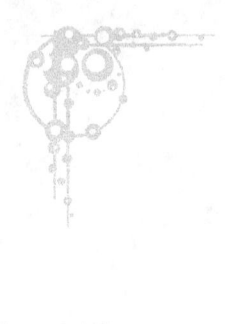

My friend said sometimes the great unknown speaks more loudly than the listener can hear. Sometimes you benefit from disconnecting from all the background noise to reacquaint yourself with yourself.

Mirror, Mirror

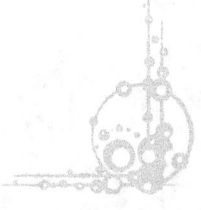

Battle Scars & Shedding Skins

He hides his feelings, to the detriment and destruction of his closest relationship, due to fear which wins.

Battle Scars & Shedding Skins

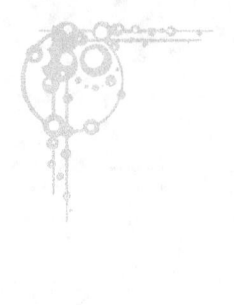
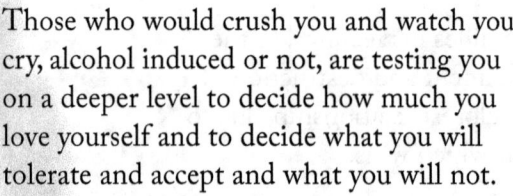

Those who would crush you and watch you cry, alcohol induced or not, are testing you on a deeper level to decide how much you love yourself and to decide what you will tolerate and accept and what you will not.

Battle Scars & Shedding Skins

The poison on the darts you
threw at me was transformed
into anti-venom and in the
process of finding my strength
I learned to laugh. Thank you.

> *Battle Scars and Shedding Skins*

Instead of taking responsibility for his behavior and actions and facing and admitting it in order to heal more than himself, he would let her slip through his fingers which were greased with pride and resentment.

Battle Scars & Shedding Skins

He didn't like her standing up for herself. Sometimes through unkind behavior toward another, masks drop and the wounds of perpetrators are revealed.

Apparently he didn't realize that manipulation and attempts to control are effective methods of self-destruction.

Battle Scars & Shedding Skins

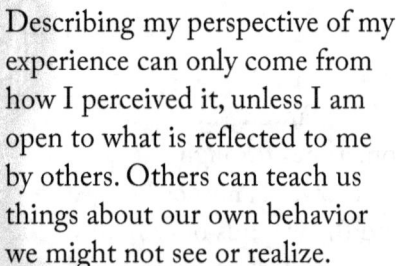

Describing my perspective of my experience can only come from how I perceived it, unless I am open to what is reflected to me by others. Others can teach us things about our own behavior we might not see or realize.

I can learn from them and from what they reflect back to me, but I must also be aware of what energy they are in, as people sometimes project their issues toward others from their unhealed wounds, even as I am working through mine.

Battle Scars & Shedding Skins

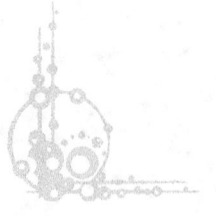

Earth school interactions with people at different levels of awakening and awareness are like a diabolical testing ground of energetic vibrations clashing against each other, where choices must be made, lessons learned and knowledge gained.

Love is how we smooth out the rough edges, heal and make it work. It's hard to love each other when or if we are attacking or judging each other or putting each other down, because of our own wounds or insecurities especially if jealousy is involved.

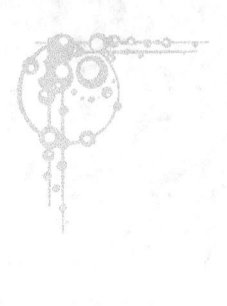

Jealousy is a scourge upon this planet. If you overcome it, you are a super hero and a powerful warrior, but it means strengthening weaknesses and insecurities, loving self, and healing wounds. We heal the collective by healing ourselves.

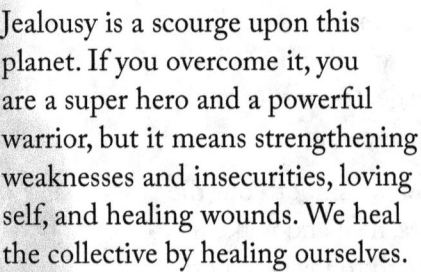

Battle Scars & Shedding Skins

From the wounds she gained much knowledge. She didn't bury the pain, she healed it and took strength from it. Perhaps the scars were like invisible armor transmuted through her own alchemy to allow love to still flow in and out.

Battle Scars & Shedding Skins

Treasure & Keys

One day she realized that it did not serve her to depend on anyone else for her happiness. It did not serve her to have expectations of anyone or anything. What she needed was within her, she just had to find it and let it out. She was her own key.

Treasure & Keys

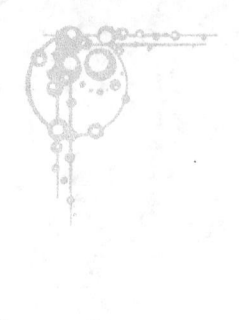

I just have to forgive you for everything, because I don't want to come back and do this dysfunction with you again.

Treasure & Keys

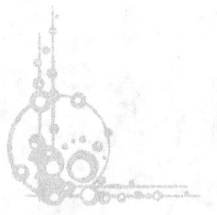

Perhaps wanting and thinking we need a balanced connection where love and honor is experienced and shared is part of the illusion, she said to herself, laughing, as she dropped flower petals along her path.

Treasure & Keys

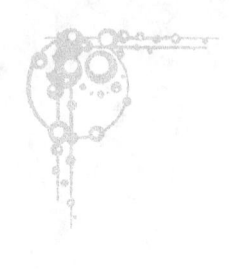
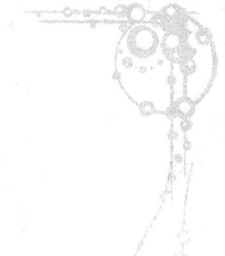

The aspects you love about her free spirit are the very reasons you cannot attempt to cage her in any way.

If you support her in the right way, she will willingly walk to the ends of the earth with you.

Treasure & Keys

It took a while for me to recognize my mistake. In ignorance I told him what is important to me because I thought it would matter to him that it mattered to me. But I soon realized what mattered to him, was knowing what to withhold from me or to use against me for control. Knowledge of what to use to manipulate and control.

Be careful about showing what matters or what hurts, because those you thought you could trust, those you love and care about the most, will often try to control or wound you due to their own unhealed wounds and fear and jealousy. It might be wise not to depend on anyone for happiness. Create it yourself and be careful whom you share it with.

Treasure & Keys

Attempting to control doesn't create power, it creates destruction.

Some people attempt to control others through jealousy and fear, perhaps through the egoic need for superiority, and maybe they succeed for a time.

But in the end, it ultimately creates their own destruction. We don't rise by manipulating others.

Treasure & Keys

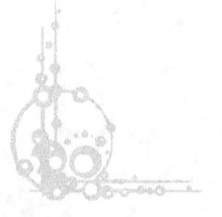

There comes a time to stop trying to protect them from what they created. Leave them where they are to learn by the experience of their free will choice.

Treasure & Keys

Blessings often come in disguise. They are for reasons known and unknown. Some are quiet treasures we hold closely to our hearts.

Treasure & Keys

If the power of forgiveness could be more deeply understood and used for our healing and liberation, the world would be a very different place.

Treasure & Keys

Suffering & Shadow

It's very sad how when people don't know what you've been through in the grueling fires of relationships, when they have not experienced the way another treated you and when you feel you must pull away from what is painful or lacking, then family and friends decide to take sides and shun you without knowing any of that. It's a huge part of what's wrong with our world. To those individuals who probably won't see this, I say piss off.

Suffering & Shadow

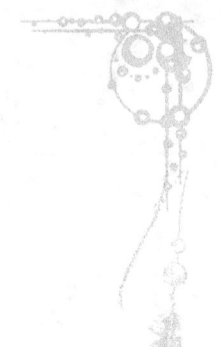

Why is it that sometimes a stranger seems to have the ability to be kinder to us than our own partner or spouse?

Why is a stranger able to exhibit more compassion for a being in a time of need that one's own partner?

Suffering & Shadow

He would twist things around and manipulate and provoke her until he broke her down to a state of crying and screaming then tell her she had issues. He tried to make her feel bad for her outburst and make her feel crazy. He would take from her and not give to her and then act like the victim and expect an apology. Fuckery 101.

Maybe he was so ignorant, that he didn't realize he was doing it time after time, for all those years. And maybe she was ignorant to stay and take it.

The projections and behavioral patterns of the wounded gas-lighting narcissist and how he preys on his victim. And even though she abhorred violence, somehow that cast iron frying pan was flying across the kitchen and made a sound like the sound of a singing bowl as it bounced off his thick skull.

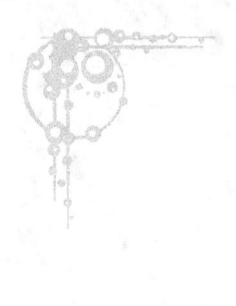

A demonstration of woman standing up for herself and taking her power back from predatory, cowardly assholes who function from outdated programs.

Suffering & Shadows

There really were no words for how peaceful one feels after cutting manipulative monsters out of their sacred space. She met a friend who made up offenses in his mind which he'd convinced himself that she had committed and then verbally attacked her for it and told many of their mutual friends what she had supposedly done. It was a test of the devil. It was a battle with darkness which was the devil in that instance and it was only a test.

He hurt her, deeply, and he knew it. And even after discussing it and supposedly making peace on both sides, after apologies and forgiveness, he would bring it up and try to use it against her again. But it wasn't truth and when she realized she didn't need to get drawn into it, that she had to leave him where he was, she had won a battle and the battle was really with herself.

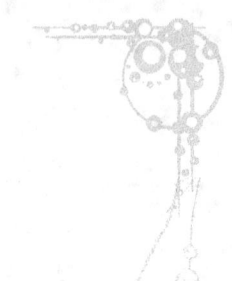

She did not need to give him or the situation her energy or concern once she recognized it for what it was. It was an aspect of a wounded child that she could not fix, but she didn't need to allow it to harm her either. Healing is an individual process and we are all doing it.

Suffering & Shadow

Perhaps monsters
create monsters.
And then there is
choice.

Suffering & Shadow

After he had been drinking all day, and it was time for dinner, the demon showed its unwelcome face, either by being easily triggered or by attempting to trigger her. So she had the choice of retreating to another part of the house and not eating dinner because it wasn't worth it to swim in that toxic alcoholic energy of him, or to stay and possibly get drawn into a verbal attack session/fight. He was pulling his old tricks out of his hat, but they didn't work anymore. (Ignorant demon and wounded host).

She saw through it and chose not to react and not get drawn into the demon's playground, which meant staying in her power and higher vibration. Those filthy looks (with daggers) he cast her way, revealed to her that he was in a gas-lighting mood.

No thank you. Those daggers are now incinerated by bitch fire before they can reach their intended target. Mama don't play that game no more. She had learned either not to make eye contact, or to look him directly in the eyes in non-reaction and change the subject before retreating from the devil's den. In others words, she was saying to the demon, 'I see you, fucker, and I'm not playing your game.

Suffering & Shadow

When facing my shadows I discovered answers to what I previously didn't understand as to why people treated me the way they did. We often do things for ourselves to try to fill a hole, but we might not be consciously aware there is or was a hole which we tried different ways to fill. People judged what I did, finding fault with it or me. It seemed like they were judging me or maybe they were judging my behavior.

In doing healing work with intuitive energy healers, they told me what they saw or what my guides showed them about me which needed to be healed or shifted. Without conscious awareness of it and the desire to fix it, I would continue to be controlled by programs I didn't even know I was running which were fed by thought loops or thought forms. I was too emotional, they said. Why? Was it a fault or a flaw? I was also very empathic which I didn't understand.

People often try to fill 'holes' with things. Little things which might make them feel happy temporarily, but they never really do fill the hole, and they become habits. Some people try to fill the hole with drugs, alcohol, relationships, material things, porn, trying to control situations or people, judging others, creating drama or picking on people and trying to make them as unhappy as they are.

I collected art and antiques and books. I decorated with them as a form of artistic expression, as a hobby. Not a crime, even though not everyone likes it. But it was a crime to me in that the things were representing or connected to emotional wounds I hadn't released and so they were holding me back to hold onto them, when they were unnecessary and in the way. I didn't know what the wounds were or how to release them, even though I had been doing much work on myself to heal from trauma or loss.

Too many books collected over the years. I used to read and read and read. And then I began to write instead. Instead of being a reader of books I became a writer of books. There were many books I knew I would never read. It was time to give some away. So I began to go through things I wasn't using and didn't need, and I gave them away, lightening my space in many ways.

I could see how I tried to fill the hole and what I did was annoying to some people who didn't understand it or me, and they would judge and the judgment felt so unfair and so hurtful. I had to learn to detach and come to place where I didn't let them bother me. It wasn't easy, but when I healed certain wounds and strengthened certain weaknesses and created healthy boundaries and enforced them, things got better.

Even though I am very compassionate and often hold space for people when others won't, that is not a license for them to be unkind to me or to dishonor me as a person. I had to learn not to allow others to work out their issues on me. I had to look more deeply at my own newly discovered wounds I didn't know I had and what I had done on some level to try to fill a void. Parts of me were neglected by myself and others. We are mirrors.

I discovered that people will find our wounds and weaknesses and use them against us and it is crushing until you get to a point that you don't care, and that is power. That is the power of detachment.

People who try to control and manipulate others will lose or destroy connections that matter to them. Some will withhold from you what they know you want and need. If you are triggered, the triggers are showing you some part yourself that needs attention, strengthening or healing.

Shadow work is never easy, because in not seeing, sensing, feeling or knowing what we really need, we often do things that bring more burdens into our lives and when we realize this, we might feel embarrassed. It's important not to hold anything against yourself, and to be aware of how important it is to release energies or thought forms that do not serve you, like, guilt, shame, unforgiveness, jealousy, resentment, etc.

Suffering & Shadow

Misperception rules this world and creates untold suffering. We suffer until we decide we no longer will.

Suffering & Shadow

Whispers from the Heart

She gave him the gift of a kiss, a gift he had never known. Even though her heart belonged to another, it was a kindness which had to be shown.

She had to show him he could be loved in spite of the darkness he'd known. She had to show him she saw beauty beyond all of that.

As we all swim through the great unknown, sometimes we take the hand of another so they can feel the love of the divine.

Whispers from the Heart

He expressed a fondness for her that was unlike anything she had ever experienced because of its raw honesty. It was something she wasn't used to. It was so refreshing.

After years of being shut out and ignored, she almost forgot what true, reflective interaction was like. Not just the reflection of another's wounds bouncing back and forth off of their walls.

It was a reflection of herself and she was curious about what she was being shown in such beautiful light. Human mirrors are fascinating. One needs to determine whether what is being reflected is oneself, or aspects of the one who is mirroring.

It can show you what is beautiful in yourself, which you were not aware of. It can show you what needs to be healed in yourself. It can show you the unhealed parts of the other or it can show you their beauty.

To see it without a mask is a rare honor. Masks will shift and fall. Look for the glimpses in between. You will discover much about yourself.

When the venom of another's wounds come flying at you, step aside and put your shields up. Keep your space clear and pure. Cleanse, release and ground and don't forget to ask your angels for help if needed.

Whispers from the Heart

It was becoming painfully apparent that she was here to teach him how she would not be treated by him. She had to muster the strength, to dig deep to find and reclaim her 'worthiness', which he didn't seem to acknowledge or reflect, due to the way he ignored her and shut her out.

She had to learn to honor herself, to step away from emotional lack and starvation and bouts of verbal abuse. When she'd had enough, she would finally walk away, into the unknown, to create and draw in something better and more nurturing for herself, for her heart and soul, which she decided she would allow herself to receive.

Within her was an incredible font of love and compassion, waiting to be shared with someone who would honor it. Maybe it was a fairy tale and maybe it existed. First, cords to the old energy must be cut. Healing work must be done. Resentment must be shed. Forgiveness must be ever present.

Love needs be sent to those who harm. Bless them, don't condemn them. They need healing, but they do not get it by harming or destroying another. Sometimes we must leave people where they are. No guilt. If beings can honor each other, if they are open to listening and changing perspectives, anything can be mended, improved or healed, but one person cannot do it for both.

Love can be starved to death, but if love is reintroduced, it can be brought back to life. Like any other living thing, it must be fed and nurtured. Anyone who ignores a garden and doesn't water it, will eventually go hungry.

Whispers from the Heart

Among the fragrant flowers and the vastness of the sky, are memories and things unremembered, of the history and the future, unfolding of you and I.

Whispers from the Heart

He placed his arms around me, pulling me into his welcome embrace and any resistance or inhibition that may have been lingering vanished into an explosion of color that was ignited as our energies combined.

He held me in a way that was like the most refreshing water for someone who was parched from crossing a barren desert alone.

Whispers from the Heart

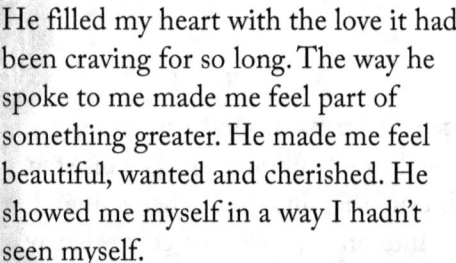

He filled my heart with the love it had been craving for so long. The way he spoke to me made me feel part of something greater. He made me feel beautiful, wanted and cherished. He showed me myself in a way I hadn't seen myself.

I got to know myself better through him and what he reflected back to me. His love helped chase away ghosts and shadows that had taken up residence in my heart. For him I am thankful. For him my heart whispers of ancient love and sings again.

Whispers From the Heart

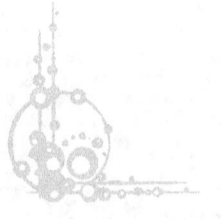

Light through the Cracks

What he saw or sensed behind
her mask was more than even
she was aware of. She didn't
fully remember who she was,
but she was beginning to, and
it was powerful, a beautiful light.

Light through the Cracks

No true God requires the sacrifice of any living being to sustain it.

Light through the Cracks

A very wise friend said when two people are going through tough relationship issues, that is the main event, and everyone else's petty judgements and nastiness about it is only a side show. Everyone has valid feelings, known or unknown.

Kudos to those who have learned to rise above judgement. Compassion is power. Peace and blessings in the gauntlet of earth school. I'm thankful for everyone on my path whether they taught me with love, patience and kindness or judgement, cruelty and ignorance. They are all teachers.

Light through the Cracks

Ignorance which rules 'darkness' is incompleteness. It lacks something. When we ignore the needs of others or ourselves, through neglect or unfairness, through selfishness or unforgiveness, through pride, ego, fear, resentment or judgment, we are existing in, feeding and being controlled by that ignorance which also infiltrates religions and politics.

Beyond that state of looping incompleteness, also understood as unworthiness, is grace. Do you remember?

Light through the Cracks

Sometimes people have misperceptions and react to limited information. It's all an illusion, we are never functioning with full knowledge of anything and it's each person's choice what to allow or not to allow.

Sometimes our own reactions are all we have control over and if we have unhealed wounds and weaknesses, we can't even control those. They control us until we strengthen and heal them.

Light through the Cracks

We learn much from behaviors, from observing behavior patterns and triggers, in ourselves and in others. Through communicating with people we learn from each other. People are mirrors and situations can be catalysts for shift and change.

The energy which messages are delivered in, might make us more or less receptive to them. Sometimes we discover that when someone dishonors us, it's showing us something we need to let go of. We must honor ourselves. Some people dishonor others due to their wounds they don't know how to heal.

Some people communicate and learn to become friends. Some people lash out from unresolved issues which create more issues. Some people poke at the wounds and weaknesses of others. (It's important to keep in mind we have to experience what we create). It's all choice. Sometimes it can be annoying and draining attempting to keep up with it, that's why it's good to take breaks. Along my ongoing healing and awakening journey have found the following to be super powers: detachment, calmness, compassion.

Light through the Cracks

Spoken from the Soul

I'm sorry I left. I'm sorry
I felt I had to leave. I'm
sorry I felt I didn't belong.

Spoken from the Soul

If you heard someone saying something unkind about another, would you defend that other if you knew it wasn't true? And what if what that person was saying about the other came from you and something you said from retaliation, hurt (real or imagined), jealousy (known or unknown), blame, old patterns, habits or programs connected to unhealed wounds or issues, even thought forms?

What if it was done because something was other than you thought it should be so you lashed out by attacking a person, even behind their back, by saying things about them which were untrue, unkind and unfair? Would you attempt to remedy, fix or mend it, even if it meant admitting that you were mistaken to the person who still holds those false thoughts and beliefs against another?

Tests reveal the warrior and the wisdom.

Spoken from the Soul

The need for connection doesn't diminish with age, in fact it might get stronger with age, but more difficult to find and/or maintain. It becomes more difficult due to pride, ego, walls, boundaries, misperceptions, expectations, preconceived ideas, wounds, expectations and attachment.

Everyone must do their own inner work. Many ignore that it's even necessary. Most find it easier to blame someone else. Nurture yourself and be open to new connections of a closer vibration than the ones which no longer work.

No one needs to feel at fault or blame when one or both cannot force a relationship to work or to continue to work. People grow and raise vibration. It's what's supposed to happen.

Spoken from the Soul

What was it about when a person speaks to someone about their experiences, wounds and stuckness? What was it to speak to friends about what we've learned and what we struggle with? An invitation to be judged or attacked...or courage through vulnerability and openness?

Does it make us a target for the wounded to fire their poison tipped arrows? Sometimes, and usually we don't realize it until it's too late, but we learn from it. It depends on what energy one is in when they are speaking of it and if what they are saying is true and if what is being said is for the purpose of understanding and healing or for the purpose of spinning yarns and falsehoods in an effort to paint someone in a bad light due to vindictiveness or revenge due to some injury, real or imagined. Reactions from limited perspectives.

Is it a heart and soul seeking answers and understanding to gain new wisdom and knowledge in order to release the effects of wounds in order to heal and move forward rather than storing it within?

Even though a person may point out the good qualities of the one who hurt them, is it some type of narcissism for them to discuss emotional and verbal abuse or neglect or disrespect? Of course it may just be one limited perspective trying to understand it, until someone gives an opinion of the side of the experience or story they hear, even if they agree that it seems dysfunctional.

There is projecting, gas lighting, not taking responsibility, deflecting, people feeling like victims and general nastiness that feels hurtful and unfair. And there is learning to detach and not to get drawn in. There is doing the work to cut cords, to take one's power back and stand in the blazing glory of it. There is strengthening weakness and healing old wounds, so that one is no longer trigged to react. That is when one can begin to see their own progress. It's all a bloody test.

Friends might help us on our path of redirection and understanding and supportiveness. Or, we might learn who our real friends really are and how wounded they are, if and when they elect to use our wounds and weaknesses against us through judgement, manipulation and control, and even targeting us in an attack or getting others to. What is the mirror of them reflecting…you or them? One must have done some inner work and have released some things to begin to be able to recognize this. Not being triggered is a sure sign of being in your strength and power.

Just because a person talks about something 'negative' as they are working it to transmute it, doesn't mean they are gossiping or being unkind, even if it's only their limited perspective and limited understanding they have to help them to heal.

Sometimes the person they would like to mend things with is not open enough to listen or to hear. When attempted, the person might turn it around and fling it back, as they refuse to be exposed in the dim light of their own shadow and the wounds they created. If they haven't faced their own shadow, they may continue to try to lay the blame elsewhere and nothing can get resolved in that energy.

Apology is hugely freeing as is forgiveness, kindness and compassion. When we can recognize the wounded state someone is functioning from, it's much easier not to feel 'offended' and when we don't feel offended we are in our power. Send love instead of negative thoughts if you wish to heal anything, including yourself. Peace.

Spoken from the Soul

The mystery in her eyes spoke
of ages now and long gone by.

Spoken from the Soul

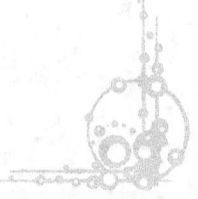

Sometimes people would say to her, 'Let it go', about unresolved issues that came up via triggers from event that molded her into who she was. The problem was that she felt like it was an ongoing process. She thought she'd let something go and some other similar, test, person or situation would come along her path to poke her and test her to do more work on that issue, or that trigger, or that feeling or that reaction. When we don't react, we know it's not an issue.

She felt she often didn't know exactly what it meant to let something go. When she had forgiven, and transmuted to create something positive from the negative, and mediated and prayed and gave thanks, it wasn't enough.

She wrote about things, burned things visualized the release of things and healing, and it wasn't enough. She gave chances to wounded people along her path, some friends, some disguised as friend which often bit her in the ass. Then later the question, 'Why didn't I notice this, or sense that?'

Sometimes we are too hard on ourselves. Sometimes we are oblivious. Sometimes we mean well and it doesn't matter. Sometimes we do our best and we are challenged to do more, to do it differently, to learn. The learning never ends. Being open to what is being shown is the key and often the challenge, as old wounds create walls and boundaries for supposed protection.

When was enough, enough? Maybe when we decide it is. Maybe when we change our thoughts and change our actions and reactions. Then our energy changes and reflects or no longer reflects these issues. Maybe when our energy is stronger and especially when what others think or say has no relevance on who we are or what we do from our hearts.

Spoken From the Soul

Beyond Belief

I must allow others to maintain and work through their beliefs, even as I release and rise above mine, because no particular limited perspective is better than any other.

They are only different levels of awakening and awareness and it's what we do with them that matters. Are they used to harm or elevate?

I also maintain the right and integrity to walk away from or rise above harmful behavior and words of others, because my wings have revealed themselves to me and they are strong and powerful.

Beyond Belief

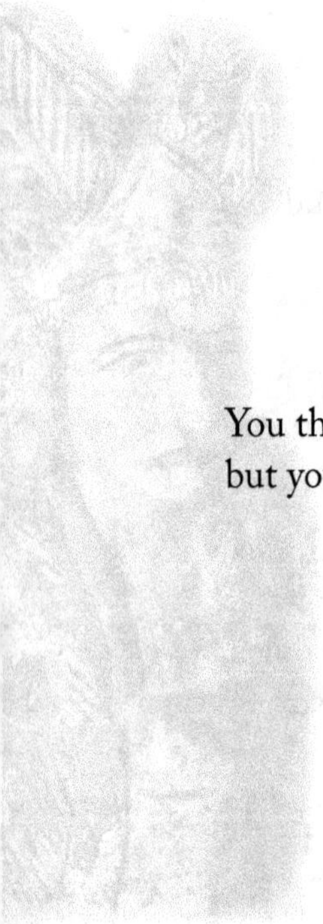

You threw me to the wolves,
but you forgot I was a dragon.

Beyond Belief

The toxic fallacy that erupted from your wounds left an indelible mark to remind me why I can never trust you to treat me with respect and honor.

When you forced me to pull away from your toxic energy, you created horror stories about me, trimmed with lies, bent on destruction and all you destroyed was something once cherished.

But that's just from my limited perspective after I cleared away the dirt you kicked in my face.

Beyond Belief

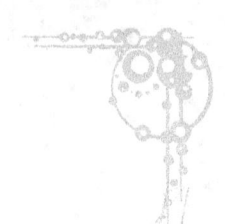

There are those who say things which sound nice, which we want to believe, and maybe they do too.

But when something comes up to test their words, they don't walk their talk. Believe what you say, or even better, move beyond belief and live the words.

Beyond Belief

In between the confusion and the knowing is a field. I will meet you there.

Beyond Belief

The flame of romance lives always within you. Tend the flame.

Beyond Belief

We don't woo simply with words. Actions must follow.

Beyond Belief

What if people loved and embraced the one who judges in themselves. Judgment comes from assuming or insisting that something is 'wrong,' when we don't know why it's happening.

The one who judges might just want to be heard. When people stop judging or condemning, they can welcome peace.

Beyond Belief

Metaphoric Light

Fading Fragments of Dreams

Fading fragments of experience,
And what knowledge there was gained,
How and why we share great love,
Through divine grace unrestrained.

How much of ourselves do we remember?
How much truth we understand?
How much have we embraced forgiveness?
For ourselves or our brother man?

Allow the fragments of ignorance to fade,
As you step into your own light,
As you face your shadow in acceptance,
In the field beyond wrong and right.

Metaphoric Light

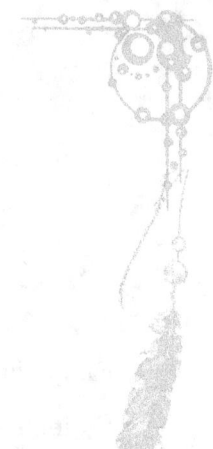

Sword fights through the centuries,
For illumination of wrong or right,
Fighting for perspectives outside of ourselves,
Creating the soul's dark night.

Use the swords to cut the ties to falsehoods,
Never do they serve,
Fill yourself with love from the highest,
To restore your radiant verve.

Metaphoric Light

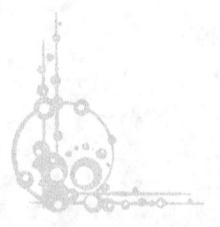

Fill your vessel with
the oil for your lamp
which is love.

Metaphoric Light

Some scholars speak of Creative Energy and Created Energy, that we are creative beings, co-creators with God.

There is part of us which always exists, the part beyond physical matter. It is said that everything created must or will be destroyed, speaking of physical matter.

It might cease to exist in this lower realm but energetically is still exists in some form. The divine element.

Metaphoric Light

Perspectives

Taking the side of one who thinks
they are a victim, doesn't always
mean they or you are right.

Perspectives

You were the jagged catalyst which
forced me to reach into the depths
of my heart and soul to find my sword
and my strength, and I did it with the
help of the angels.

Thank you for kicking me off that cliff
so I could discover my forgotten wings
and fly.

Perspectives

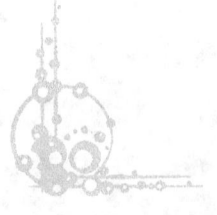

It's the pain which tells the most poignant stories. It rises from the depths in search of the light.

Perspectives

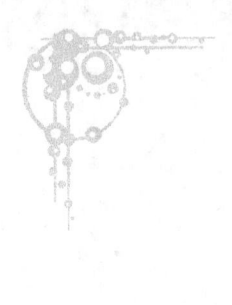

Focusing on what others are doing, and judging it, often takes the focus away from what we need to be healing in ourselves. Breaking habits breaks us out of shells.

Perspectives

It's not about making others wrong or making them look bad. That might be ego trying to feel superior. If people cannot disconnect from their addictions to certain things, they will continue to suffer and create more suffering.

Addicted to the news and political ideologies. Addicted to their particular religions (many of which encourage hate and judgement). Wanting to be 'right'. Feeding wars.

There are many things which are 'right' to different people at different levels of awakening and awareness. Closed perspectives are coffins of ignorance.

Perspectives

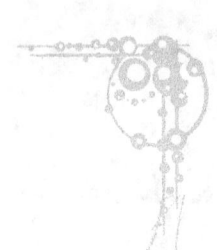

Global peace must come from within each person individually and not by controlling anyone else, not by ideologies or expectation or ego.

Perspectives

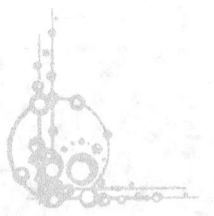
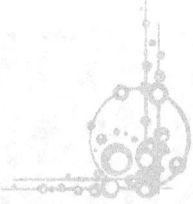

Sometimes certain types of love seemed unattainable or unsustainable. It seemed like it was only a fairy take thanks to unhealed wounds, fears and ego.

Usually two people are not functioning at the same vibrational levels and so obstacles present along with misunderstanding due to misperception. Life is skewed by masks and veils.

But whatever love I can image or need already exists within me. Others reflect it back to me sometimes, which fills my heart with gratitude

Perspectives

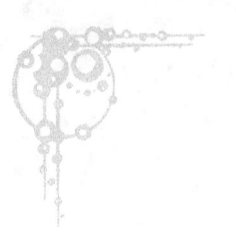

There are types of judgment many don't even realize are types of judgment, which keep us stuck, take our power and cause us to withhold hold love from ourselves.

What we think about, talk about, Or hold onto because it feels hurtful or unfair...those are types of judgments. And until we learn to let them go, they will keep coming back to test us.

Perspectives

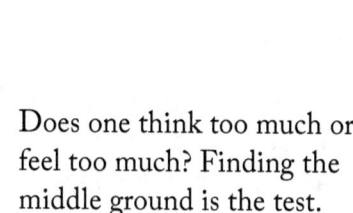

Does one think too much or feel too much? Finding the middle ground is the test.

Perspectives

> We shouldn't just blame other people for things we probably don't understand, we should pay attention to your own reactions which will show us things about ourselves.
>
> *Perspectives*

Teachers aren't always people with degrees in classrooms. Teachers are beings who are able to show us something is such a light, good or bad, that we learn something valuable or necessary from it. We are always students of life.

Everyone and everything is our teacher. It is through inquisitiveness and openness that we learn. If are closed off, life will find a way to crack us open, for the light to get in and out.

Perspectives

About the Author

Janine Palmer (Spirit Silver Moon) grew up in Northern California and resides in Utah today. After devastating county-wide wild fires in Southern California and global economic collapse, Janine and her family endured physical, economical and emotional losses, along with the loss of friendships. Judgmental treatment by so-called religious people (family/friends) caused her to question religions due to poor treatment by others in religious ideology. These initiations tested her inner strength and caused her to investigate more deeply for truth, what brings true happiness, forward movement, the evolvement of the soul and ultimately she discovered her calling.

She was a phoenix who rose from her own ashes with a powerful story to share of truth, strength, wisdom, compassion, love and taking one's power back. We must remember our magnificence to in order to rise above so much illusion. Looking for answers, Janine Palmer (Silver Moon) extensively studied and continues to study multiple healing modalities for emotional and spiritual healing.

Janine has studied World Religions, Spirituality, Early Christianity, Gnosticism, Philosophy, Critical Thinking,

Biblical Scholars, and Spiritual teachers. Janine is a Clinical Hypnotherapist and Shamanic Practitioner. In the spiritual and emotional arenas, Janine has studied and become certified in the following areas: Cognitive Behavioral Hypnotherapy, Ericksonian Hypnosis, Energy Psychology, Emotional Freedom Technique (EFT or Tapping), Kinesiology, Muscle Testing, Neuro-linguistic Programming (NLP) the language of the mind, Reiki Master and Gamma Healing for overcoming energy vampires, healing emotional traumas, anxiety, depression and PTSD, and Shamanic Journey Work.

These modalities are helpful for releasing stress, old pain, resentment, anger, doubt, grief, unforgiveness or anything which blocks forward movement. Through her healing sessions, whether held in person, via phone or skype, she has helped others heal, grow, overcome obstacles and move forward lighter after releasing what no longer serves. This knowledge and wisdom is contained within her writings of uplifting messages for healing. She shares tools we can use to assist ourselves and others on their path. Janine is the author of multiple books containing many genres and messages from various teachings and modalities. The four main genres are story poems, romance, rising above dogma and emotional and spiritual healing. These are presented as poetic tales which have received very positive support and feedback around the world.

Janine's compassion and calling to help others break free of limiting and painful situations can be felt through the writings contained her he book series Divine Heretic. She does God's work for humanity, for the collective and greater good. It is a gift and a blessing she is very grateful for.

Visit Janine's web pages

www.HarmonyEnergyHealing.com
www.DivineHereticBooks.com

www.ingramcontent.com/pod-product-compliance
Lightning Source LLC
Chambersburg PA
CBHW052020070526
44584CB00016B/1828